DAYS THAT SHOOK THE WORLD

THE MOON LANDING

20 JULY 1969

Paul Mason

W HODDER Wayland

an imprint of Hodder Children's Books

DAYS THAT SHOOK THE WORLD

Assassination in Sarajevo   The Dream of Martin Luther King
D-Day   The Fall of the Berlin Wall
Hiroshima   The Kennedy Assassination
Pearl Harbor   The Moon Landing
The Chernobyl Disaster   The Wall Street Crash

Produced by Monkey Puzzle Media Ltd
Gissing's Farm, Fressingfield
Suffolk IP21 5SH, UK

First published in 2002 by Hodder Wayland
An imprint of Hodder Children's Books
Text copyright © 2002 Hodder Wayland
Volume copyright © 2002 Hodder Wayland
This paperback edition published in 2003

Series Concept: Liz Gogerly
Editor: Jason Hook
Design: Jane Hawkins
Picture Researcher: Lynda Lines
Consultant: Michael Rawcliffe

Cover picture: Buzz Aldrin on the moon.
Title page picture: Buzz Aldrin descends from the lunar capsule to the moon.

We are grateful to the following for permission to reproduce photographs:
Corbis 8 (Bettmann), 9 (Bettmann), 10, 11 left (Bettmann), 13 top, 13 bottom (Bettmann), 16 (Bettmann), 17 (NASA/Roger Ressmeyer), 20, 21 both (Bettmann), 24 bottom (NASA), 29 (NASA), 30 (Bettmann), 32 (Bettmann), 34 (Bettmann), 35 top (Bettmann), 40 (Shelly Katz), 41 (Bettmann); MPM Images front cover, title page, 26, 27, 39 both, 42; NASA 6, 7, 11 right, 14, 18, 19, 23, 25 both, 28 right, 31, 33 both, 38, 46; Rex Features 15 top (Dalmas), 22, 24 top (Stills), 28 left, 35 bottom, 36, 37; Science Photo Library 12 (David A Hardy); Topham Picturepoint 15 bottom (AP), 43.

Printed and bound in Italy by G. Canale & C.Sp.A, Turin.

British Library Cataloguing in Publication Data
Mason, Paul
The moon landing. - (Days that shook the world)
1.Space flight to the moon - Juvenile literature
I.Title
629.4'5

ISBN 07502 3578 0

Hodder Children's Books
A division of Hodder Headline Limited
338 Euston Road, London NW1 3BH

CONTENTS

"WE HAVE A LIFT-OFF"   6

THE RACE FOR SPACE   8

THE ATOMIC BOMB   10

SOVIETS IN SPACE   12

MERCURY   14

THE USA AWAKES   16

THE APOLLO PROGRAMME   18

THE ASTRONAUTS   20

FROM THE EARTH TO THE MOON   22

20 JULY 1969 — "THE EAGLE HAS LANDED"   24

20 JULY 1969 — "ONE SMALL STEP"   26

20 JULY 1969 — MOON DUST   28

THE PERFECT PICTURE   30

SPLASHDOWN   32

THE SPACE AGE   34

APOLLO 13   36

THE END OF THE SPACE RACE   38

WHAT IF ... ?   40

LEGACY   42

GLOSSARY, FURTHER INFORMATION   44

TIMELINE   46

INDEX   47

It is 4.15 am, on Wednesday 16 July 1969. Astronauts Neil Armstrong, Edwin 'Buzz' Aldrin and Michael Collins wake up, knowing that today is a special day. There is a good chance that they are about to make history, by becoming the first people ever to land on the moon. If they are successful, their names will never be forgotten. But there is a possibility that, if something goes wrong, the breakfast they are about to eat will be their last.

Undeterred, the three men launch into a meal of steak and eggs, then put on their special clothing and spacesuits (the shock-absorbing material in the suits is used today in the soles of trainers). All around the launch site at the Kennedy Space Center in Florida,

technicians and engineers are making last-minute checks to the equipment. There are so many different parts in the rocket that the National Aeronautics and Space Administration (NASA) has had to come up with a new way of identifying them. Each part is bar-coded, just like groceries in supermarkets today.

Outside the Space Center are gathered well over a million people. Many of them have come from hundreds, even thousands, of miles away in the hope of seeing history being made. The launch area itself is cordoned off from the public, but all around the Space Center every available public space contains part of the huge crowd of spectators. On this particular Wednesday, people have arranged to visit friends they

The crew of Apollo 11 were, from left to right, Neil Armstrong, Michael Collins and 'Buzz' Aldrin.

have not seen in years, come to stay in seedy motels, camped in tents on the beach, even slept in their cars – anything to have the chance to see Apollo 11 lift off.

All around the world, millions more people are glued to their television sets. It is one of the first ever live international television events. Everybody's attention is focused on the huge Saturn 5 rocket that will blast the Apollo spacecraft into the sky. It is filled with 2,000 tonnes of explosive rocket fuel, and the astronauts are inside. With sixty seconds to go all checks are complete, and the countdown continues.

'Five ... four ... three ... two ... one ... zero. All engines running.' The whole world holds its breath; can the mission to the moon succeed? There is a tremendous rumbling noise. 'Lift-off. We have a lift-off.' Burning fifteen tonnes of fuel every second, the Saturn 5 rocket rises from the launch pad. Within moments it is high in the sky. Humankind's attempt to reach another world is under way.

The Saturn 5 rocket blasts the Apollo 11 spacecraft away from the launch pad at Kennedy Space Center, and the historic journey to the moon begins.

A TV Event

" My father bought our new TV set specially to watch America try to reach the moon. Not too many people had [one] where we lived ... it was quite an event, all gathered around – family, friends, neighbours, everyone – waiting for the rocket to take off. I remember thinking at the time how there were people all round the world watching the exact same pictures. "

Mary-Lou Jackson remembers waiting for Apollo 11 to lift off during her childhood in Arkansas, USA.

THE STORY OF THE Apollo 11 mission starts many years before the rocket took off from the Kennedy Space Center. The idea of travelling to the moon had existed for centuries, but one of the first semi-scientific versions of how to get there appeared in a novel written by the French author Jules Verne. Published in 1865, it was titled *From The Earth To The Moon*, and contained Verne's thoughts on how powerful a cannon one would need to fire a craft to the moon.

Verne's idea was nonsense, of course, but it inspired early rocket pioneers all round the world. Several men began to think that perhaps it would be possible to send a rocket, rather than a missile from a giant cannon, to the moon. One of them was the American Dr Robert Goddard, who in 1926 became the first person to launch a liquid-fuelled rocket.

Despite Goddard's achievements, rocket development during the 1920s and '30s was most successful in

Robert Goddard (1882–1945)

The American physicist Robert Goddard (1882–1945) studied and taught at Clark University in Massachusetts, but he made his earliest rocket experiments in his spare time and with his own money. The government of Massachusetts once told him to conduct his research outside the state because it was thought to be so dangerous! Goddard is most famous for having fired, on 16 March 1926, the world's first liquid-fuelled rocket.

Germany. By 1932 the German Rocket Society had launched eighty-seven experimental flights. When the Nazis came to power in Germany in 1933, Robert Ley – one of the Society's leading members – emigrated to the USA. Another key member, named Wernher von Braun, stayed in Germany and was put to work on weapon development by the Nazi leader Adolf Hitler.

During the Second World War, von Braun developed a rocket-powered weapon called the V2. It travelled faster than the speed of sound and took just six minutes to reach London from a launch base in Peenemunde on Germany's Baltic coast. At the time of Germany's surrender, in May 1945, von Braun was working on a series of even more powerful rockets which were designed to be launched at the USA from the west coast of France.

At the launch of the first V2, on 3 October 1942, the Nazi military commander Walter Dornberger had turned to von Braun and said: 'Do you realize what we have done? Today the spaceship is born.'

At the end of the war, von Braun and his team of rocket scientists surrendered to American forces. They hoped that they would be able to continue their work by helping the USA develop a rocket-based space programme. Von Braun and his scientists went to work at the US Army's testing centre in White Sands, New Mexico. But for many years the American government was to ignore the challenge of space and give the building of rockets a low priority. It would be some time before the USA developed a space programme to match the one of von Braun's imagination.

Wernher von Braun sits beside a model rocket in 1955, a decade after he came to the USA.

A massive mushroom cloud rises above an atomic bomb set off at Bikini Atoll in the Pacific Ocean in 1954.

THE SECOND WORLD WAR ended in 1945 with the unconditional surrender of Japan, Germany's powerful ally. The Japanese had been forced to surrender after a new and terrible weapon was used against their homeland. Dropped on the cities of Hiroshima then Nagasaki, the atomic bomb was the most destructive weapon ever made. With it, army commanders could lay waste whole cities without putting at risk a single one of their own soldiers.

Although they had been allies during the war, the Soviet Union and the USA soon became deadly enemies. Much of the world became divided into countries that supported one or the other of these two 'superpowers'. At first, only the USA and its allies had the atomic bomb, and they tried to keep the secret of its manufacture from the Soviet Union. Although they controlled vast areas of territory surrounding their borders, the Soviets were vulnerable to an atomic

bomb dropped from an aeroplane. Their leaders resolved to develop weapons technology to match that of their enemies.

By 1949 the Soviets not only had their own atomic bombs, but had also gained an important advantage over the USA. As early as August 1933 a rocket scientist named Sergei Korolev had launched a rocket that reached a height of over 400 metres. Three months later, a Soviet rocket had soared for almost five kilometres. Korolev would later design the rocket that launched Sputnik 1, the world's first satellite, into space. The Soviet Union's military commanders could see that by attaching an atomic bomb to a powerful rocket, they would have an amazingly powerful weapon. In contrast, the USA was always behind in rocket technology. By 1935 Robert Goddard had managed to get a rocket to reach 2.3 kilometres – less than half the height a Soviet rocket had achieved two years earlier.

By the mid-1950s both the USA and the Soviet Union had developed intercontinental ballistic missiles (ICBMs) – rocket-powered missiles that had a range of over 8,000 kilometres. Atomic bombs were being made smaller, and could be fitted inside these missiles. Rockets carrying nuclear warheads could now be launched from submarines, which by lying hidden off an enemy's coast could dramatically increase the range of atomic bombs. Soon practically the whole world was within striking distance of an attack with atomic weapons.

But neither superpower could use its weapons. If they did, the other side would launch their own atomic missiles, threatening the entire world with destruction. The superpowers remained permanently on the brink of war, without actually fighting – a period in history known as the Cold War.

Sergei Korolev, the Soviet Union's most successful rocket scientist.

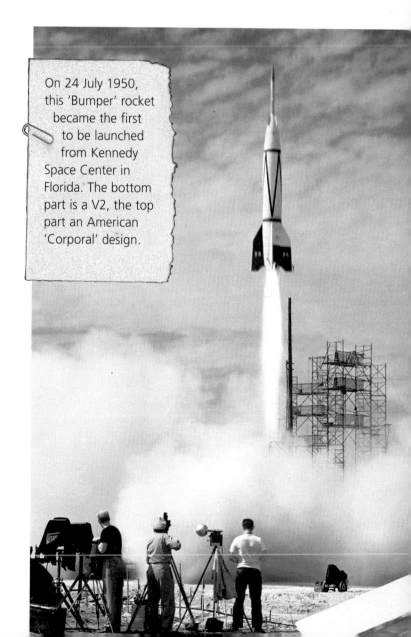

On 24 July 1950, this 'Bumper' rocket became the first to be launched from Kennedy Space Center in Florida. The bottom part is a V2, the top part an American 'Corporal' design.

The Iron Curtain

Soon after the end of the Second World War, Europe became divided into two. On one side were the democratic, capitalist countries of the West, allied to the USA. On the other were the communist countries of the East, led by the Soviet Union. Winston Churchill christened this division the 'Iron Curtain'. The champions of East and West, the Soviet Union and the USA, became challengers in the 'space race', with the moon as the finishing post.

AFTER THE END OF the Second World War, the USA's development of rocketry lagged behind the Soviet Union every step of the way. By 1955 the Soviets had developed a missile – the R-7 – which was powerful enough to reach the American mainland or put a satellite into orbit. The USA was three years or more behind, and it was not until 1958 that its first ICBM was tested. The American government seemed to give rocket research a low priority. As the Soviets continued to develop their technology, Wernher von Braun struggled with little money and plenty of government restrictions. But then the USA got the wake-up call it needed.

On 4 October 1957 the Soviet government announced that it had launched its first satellite, named Sputnik 1 (sputnik is Russian for 'fellow traveller'). The USA went into a state of shock.

American citizens had always felt that the Pacific Ocean to the west and the Atlantic Ocean to the east protected their homeland from attack. Now a Soviet satellite was orbiting the earth, and it crossed the USA every hour. People suddenly felt vulnerable to the Soviet threat.

The American president Dwight D Eisenhower tried to play down the significance of Sputnik 1, saying that he had 'no interest in an outer space basketball game'. He meant that space was a diversion that had no impact on the real world. But people were not reassured. In fact, Eisenhower's words made them think that he was getting old and out of touch. Then the Soviet Union launched another rocket into space, this time carrying a living creature – Laika the dog, who became the first space traveller.

Even now, the USA's humiliation was not complete. In December 1957 the US Navy, stung into action by the Soviet successes, tried to launch a Vanguard rocket that would put a satellite weighing under two kilograms into orbit. The attempt seemed faintly pathetic, given that the Sputnik satellite had weighed

This artwork shows Sputnik 1. The satellite had four radio antennae which sent signals back to earth from space.

President Eisenhower of the USA meets Soviet leader Nikita Khrushchev in 1950. While Khrushchev developed powerful rockets, Eisenhower felt matters on earth were more important.

over ninety kilograms. Wernher von Braun, who worked for the Army's rocket research group, later said: 'We are competing [with the Soviet Union] only in spirit.' The world's press nonetheless gathered to watch the Vanguard rocket take off. Instead they saw it explode on the launch pad. The *London Daily Herald* headline ran: 'Oh, What A Flopnik'. The Soviets called it Kaputnik. The USA's attempts to get into space were becoming a joke.

American embarrassment in 1957 stirred an aggressive reaction. On 1 October 1958 the National Aeronautics and Space Administration (NASA) was created to co-ordinate American space research. Space went from being a subject of rivalry between the Army and the Navy to being a national concern. But even as NASA was being created, the Soviet Union was launching probes that were headed for the moon itself. The Americans were still a very long way behind.

Laika the Space Dog

Laika was a female dog launched into orbit by the Soviet Union in November 1957. She was the first living creature ever to go into outer space, and her Sputnik 2 capsule contained equipment for measuring her pulse, respiration, blood pressure and heartbeat. Laika was kept alive for ten days to prove that it was physically possible to survive the conditions of outer space. Unfortunately for Laika, no one had worked out how to get her down again. The capsule was not designed to return to earth, and Laika died in space.

Looking like they have just stepped off the set of a low-budget science-fiction movie, these seven men are actually the original Mercury astronauts.

O N 9 APRIL 1959, the new NASA organization revealed a space programme that captured the imagination of the American public. It was called Mercury, and was intended to put the first men into outer space. The Mercury programme had seven astronauts taking part, and finally the public had faces to which they could relate. The astronauts were from a military background, and had flown combat missions in the Second World War and the Korean War. They seemed to embody a combative American spirit that might at last put the USA ahead in the space race. The press praised their bravery – no one had forgotten the recent image of an unmanned US rocket exploding on the launch pad.

Only Eisenhower, it seemed, was unimpressed. Even after John F Kennedy was elected president in 1960 on a promise to 'get America moving again', Eisenhower continued to question the use of huge amounts of government money in what he called 'a mad effort to win a stunt race'.

Yuri Gagarin signs autographs for his many admirers.

White House just three months when the Soviet Union made a startling announcement – they had beaten the USA again. On 12 April 1961, the Soviet astronaut Yuri Gagarin had been launched into orbit. He became the first human to go to outer space. He was hailed as a hero in the Soviet Union, not only because of his amazing achievement, but also as a symbol of the Soviet Union's ability to humiliate the USA.

When the announcement of Gagarin's success was made, a journalist telephoned NASA's spokesperson, Lieutenant Colonel 'Shorty' Powers, at 3.00 am in the morning to ask for a comment. Powers' reply was brief and unintentionally to the point: 'If you want anything from us, you jerk, the answer is we're all asleep!'

A month later the USA started to wake up when Alan Shepard made a 490-kilometre sub-orbital flight in his Freedom 7 capsule. But nothing could hide the fact that Shepard's flight had lasted just fifteen minutes – Gagarin's Vostok capsule, in comparison, had circled the world. Things were about to change, though, as the USA began to put all its scientific and technological resources behind winning the space race.

Reaction to Gagarin

" When Gagarin came down there was a tremendous reception ... in the Kremlin. There must have been about 6,000 people ... The next day we had to drive to Leningrad, about 700 km from Moscow. They were starting to fill my [car with petrol] and the automation had gone wrong so they were having to do it by hand. And a jeep from a nearby farm came along and was waiting, and the two chaps were talking to each other. And one said, 'Well, there you are, this is our Russia all over. Yesterday, we celebrate the first man in space; today, we can't even fill the tank of the British ambassador.' "

Sir Frank Roberts, British Ambassador to Moscow 1960–62.

President Kennedy christened his government's policies the 'New Frontier'. The phrase contained a clear reference to the challenge of the stars, the last frontier of human exploration, and especially to the race to get a human into space. But Kennedy had been in the

Gagarin's flight was the wake-up call the USA needed. A month later Alan Shepard, shown here posing for the camera, became the first American in space.

On 25 May 1961, President Kennedy set a target for the USA: 'I believe this nation should commit itself to achieving the goal, before this decade is out, of landing a man on the moon and returning him safely to earth. No single space project in this period will be more impressive to mankind.'

IN EFFECT THE PRESIDENT was saying that nothing that had happened before counted – what people would remember best was who had placed the first man on the moon. Kennedy was right, as history would show.

Between Alan Shepard's flight in May 1961 and the end of the Mercury programme in 1963, American astronauts made six flights. John Glenn became the first American into orbit in February 1962, and the final Mercury flight orbited the globe twenty-two times. NASA now knew it could send men into space,

but there were still many obstacles to overcome before a man could land on the moon. A spacecraft would have to dock with another in space (crucial if a smaller ship were to visit the moon and then rejoin a larger one for the journey home). An astronaut would have to be able to leave his spacecraft and work outside it. Tests would also have to be carried out to see if the human body could survive for long periods in space.

After Mercury came the Gemini programme. This achieved the next steps in the space programme's progress with remarkable speed, in the course of nine missions flown between March 1965 and November 1966. The first American space walk took place when Ed White stepped from Gemini 4 in June 1966. At this time the Soviet Union was pursuing the Luna programme of unmanned missions to the moon. But it was the USA that was making the greatest strides towards sending a man there.

President John F Kennedy in September 1962 at the NASA centre in Houston, Texas. He had recently promised an audience at Rice University that the USA would beat the Soviet Union to the moon.

Two spacecraft carry out the docking procedure for the first time, as Gemini 6 docks with Gemini 7 in December 1965.

Gemini 5 set a new record, orbiting earth 120 times and allowing scientists to study the effects of space on the human body. Finally, Gemini 6 and 7 successfully docked while in orbit. The remaining Gemini missions polished these procedures, and during Gemini 12's flight astronaut Buzz Aldrin left the spacecraft and worked outside it for five hours.

At the same time, Wernher von Braun was working on a huge rocket called Saturn 5. This was essentially a giant version of the V2 with which the Nazis had tried to defeat Britain, and it had to be powerful enough to carry humans out of earth's orbit. Other scientists were working on a craft called the lunar module – which would eventually land astronauts on the moon. The pieces were starting to fall into place.

Kennedy on the Space Race

"If we are to win the battle that is going on around the world between freedom and tyranny, if we are to win the battle for men's minds, the dramatic achievements in space which occurred in recent weeks should have made clear to us ... the impact of [the space race] on the minds of men everywhere ... We go into space because whatever mankind must undertake, free men must fully share."

Part of Kennedy's special address to Congress, 25 May 1961, following Gagarin's flight. He was describing the importance of the space race as part of the conflict between democracy and communism.

17

Apollo 7 lifts off in spectacular style. This was the first manned Apollo flight to be launched successfully.

THE APOLLO PROGRAMME WAS meant to be the final stage of NASA's effort to put a human being on the moon. But it suffered early setbacks when many changes had to be made to the initial design of the teardrop-shaped spacecraft. Then, on 27 January 1967, tragedy struck. During a practice countdown for Apollo 1, a spark lit the pure oxygen inside the spacecraft. Apollo 1 burst into flames, and the crewmen Gus Grissom, Ed White and Roger Chafee were killed instantly. It would be nineteen months before a manned Apollo flight left the ground.

On 9 November 1967 there was better news. The giant Saturn 5 rocket was launched carrying the unmanned Apollo 4 capsule – the rocket to launch the trip to the moon was now ready. NASA made two more unmanned flights before Apollo 7 was successfully launched with a human crew. But with just one manned flight completed, NASA had fallen behind schedule. They had to get the programme back on track.

NASA made a tremendous leap forward with Apollo 8, the first manned mission to be launched on a Saturn 5 rocket. Apollo 8 took astronauts James A Lovell, Frank Borman and William A Anders on a flight around the moon. They did not land there, but they were the first people ever to see – rather than imagine – the earth as a planet. Their spacecraft orbited the moon on Christmas Eve, 1968, beaming back television pictures of the blue-and-white earth against the dark background of space.

The Apollo programme continued to make progress. Apollo 9 became the first mission to take along a lunar module, a capsule which successfully separated from the command module and returned while in orbit around the earth. Apollo 10 performed the same procedure, but in orbit around the moon. NASA now knew it had the pieces in place for a successful visit to the moon. The Saturn 5 rocket was powerful enough to launch the mission. The lunar module was able to leave its control module and return successfully. It

This is the amazing moment in time when an astronaut first saw the earth rise above the surface of the moon. The picture was taken from Apollo 8 by astronaut William Anders.

A Moment in Time

On Christmas Eve, 1968, the three astronauts on board Apollo 8 complete an orbit of the moon. They become the first human beings to see the dark side of the moon, and the first to circle a celestial body other than the earth. But they must spend Christmas with the earth a distant blue planet. They send home the message: 'Good night, good luck, a Merry Christmas, and God bless all of you ... on the good earth.'

was also now known to be possible for people to survive long periods in space then return safely to earth. The only thing NASA did not know was whether the lunar module could land on the moon and then relaunch itself. The only way to find out was to try it and see.

Neil Armstrong, the mission commander for Apollo 11's attempt to land on the moon.

On Monday 6 January 1969, astronaut Neil Armstrong was called into the office of Deke Slayton, NASA's director of Flight Crew Operations. Slayton told him that his crew would be flying the Apollo 11 mission. But that was not all – Armstrong was told that Apollo 11 would be the spacecraft that attempted the first moon landing in history.

The pilot of the lunar module would be Buzz Aldrin, a brilliant scientist and ex-fighter pilot. He was nicknamed 'Mr Rendezvous' by the other astronauts because he had helped design the method of docking one spacecraft with another. The command module would be manned by Michael Collins, who would continue to orbit the moon while Aldrin and Armstrong attempted to make the landing in the lunar module. When they returned, the command module would carry them safely back to earth.

Collins was the only crew member of Apollo 11 who knew he would not walk on the moon, even if the mission was successful. But he thought that in some ways his experience of journeying alone to the dark side of the moon would be unique. 'If a count were taken,' he said, 'the score would be three billion plus two over on the other side of the moon, and one plus God knows what over on this side.'

Almost immediately, the astronauts began training for their mission. They spent hour after hour in a flight simulator. This was an exact copy of the spacecraft they would fly to the moon and back, and all the dials and gauges behaved in the same way as those on board the real Apollo 11. At first the astronauts simply became familiar with the controls, but gradually their instructors made things more difficult. Suddenly an oxygen tank would spring a leak, or one of the pressure gauges would start to fall. Any one of a thousand things that might go wrong during the flight would be simulated. In this way, the astronauts practised what they might have to do for real – fixing any problem that put their mission to the moon in jeopardy.

SINCE THE BEGINNING OF its exploration of space, NASA had used the same way of selecting crews for its missions. Each crew of three astronauts had a back-up team of three, who were ready to take over if there was a problem with the first crew. The back-up team then missed two missions before becoming the main crew for the next one. So, the team that backed up Apollo 8 would be the main crew for the Apollo 11 mission.

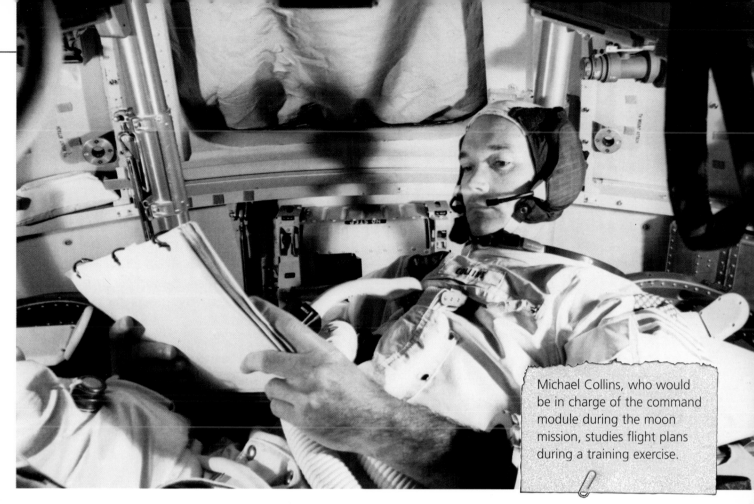

Michael Collins, who would be in charge of the command module during the moon mission, studies flight plans during a training exercise.

Neil Armstrong (1930–)

Neil Armstrong earned his pilot's licence at the age of sixteen and joined the US Navy in 1949. He flew seventy-eight combat missions during the Korean War, before returning home to study for degrees in aeronautical and aerospace engineering. Armstrong worked as a test pilot, flying rocket-powered planes, before joining NASA in 1962. He was a modest man, who said: 'If historians are fair, they won't see this flight like Lindbergh's. They'll recognise that the landing is only one small part of a large programme.' (Charles Lindbergh in 1927 had made the first non-stop solo transatlantic flight.)

Buzz Aldrin, who would navigate the lunar module to its landing site on the moon, looks at pictures of possible landing places.

THE LIFT-OFF OF Apollo 11 on Wednesday 16 July 1969, was watched by 7,000 official guests, including vice-president Spiro Agnew and former president Lyndon B Johnson. People in the guest stands wore dark sunglasses or held hats up to the sky to shield their eyes from the bright Florida sunshine. History was about to be made.

8.32 am (All times given are those at Mission Control, Houston) The stage-one rockets that powered the huge Saturn 5 fired up, and – incredibly slowly at first – the moon mission finally got under way. As the rocket left the ground, television viewers heard a voice from Mission Control in Houston, Texas, say: 'We have a lift-off!'

8.34 am After only two minutes, the first stage of the mission was complete.

Having done their job, the stage-one rockets fell away from the rest of Apollo 11. The mission had now reached a height of seventy kilometres, and the stage-two rockets kicked in. They burnt for seven minutes before also dropping away. Apollo 11 was travelling at over 36,000 kilometres per hour. The stage-three rockets now burnt for two-and-a-half minutes before shutting down, by which time Apollo 11 was travelling in orbit around the earth at an astonishing speed of over 41,000 kilometres per hour.

11.30 am After nearly three hours orbiting the earth, Apollo 11 set its course for the moon. The stage-three rockets ignited again for nearly six minutes. This thrust Apollo 11 out of the pull of earth's gravity, and Armstrong sent back a message to Mission Control: 'That Saturn gave us a magnificent ride.'

The former American president Lyndon B Johnson is at the centre of the crowd watching Apollo 11's lift-off. You can tell from all the sunglasses what a sunny day it was.

Apollo 11 streaks across the sky at the beginning of its journey to the moon. All that the world can do now is wait and see if the mission succeeds.

11.49 am Michael Collins ignited rockets which separated his command module from the lunar module. The two craft drifted in space until, once they were twenty-three metres apart, Collins began the complicated and delicate manoeuvre of docking with the lunar module. This was the final checking procedure – the astronauts and their spaceship were now ready for their journey to the moon. They ate their first meal – chicken salad, sweet apple sauce and shrimp cocktail – and tested their television camera to make sure it was working.

Now all that the astronauts could do was settle down and try to get some rest. There were no beds on the spacecraft, so they just slid into their sleeping bags and slept however they could. When they arrived in the moon's orbit in three days time, Armstrong, Collins and Aldrin would need all their wits about them – to make a successful landing on the moon.

Hard to Believe

" We turned on the television straight after lunch and sat watching the preparations. I suppose they had been ready for a long time: there didn't seem to be much activity by the time we tuned in. My two-year-old son Paul was just big enough to get caught up in the excitement, although he doesn't remember it now. I remember it was a fine, bright day, and there were over a million people watching the launch. As they lifted off I remember thinking that it couldn't be real; those men couldn't really be going to the moon. "

Housewife Marie Gaylard, recalling watching Apollo 11's lift-off on television.

Apollo 11's command module, called Columbia, orbits the moon.

Michael Collins, Columbia's pilot, told Armstrong and Aldrin: 'You cats take it easy on the lunar surface.' Then he pressed the button to separate the two craft, with the words: 'Okay, there you go! Beautiful!' After checking for damage to the Eagle's landing gear as it drifted away, Collins told Armstrong: 'I think you've got a fine-looking flying machine there.' Eagle now began its 96-kilometre descent to the moon.

12.18 pm Just after midday, on Sunday 20 July 1969, the Apollo 11 astronauts prepared to separate the lunar module, named Eagle, from the command module, named Columbia.

3.06 pm As the lunar module approached to within twelve kilometres of the moon's surface, an alarm suddenly sounded. The computer was flashing up the code 1202, warning Armstrong that something was wrong. In all the simulations this had never happened before, and Armstrong knew only that it meant the computer was overloaded. After a tense wait, Mission Control radioed with information – as long as the computer alarm was beeping, not continuous, the mission could continue.

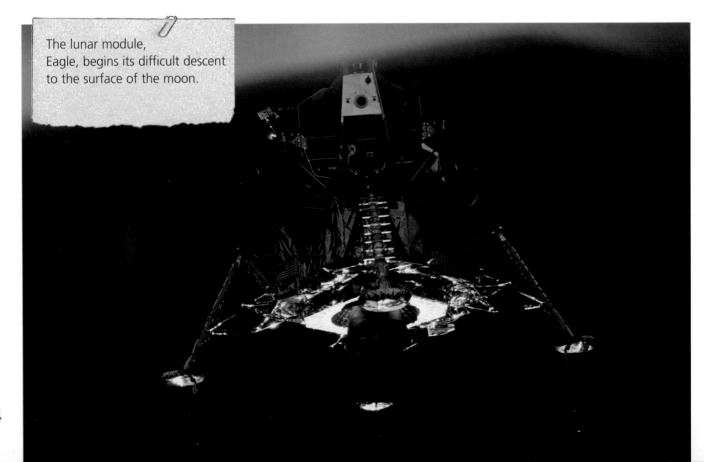

The lunar module, Eagle, begins its difficult descent to the surface of the moon.

The Apollo 11 mission badge shows an eagle landing on the moon.

Mission Control celebrates, as Eagle touches down successfully on the surface of the moon.

At 900 metres from the moon, the alarms came back on again. Still the Eagle swooped down, until it was just 300 metres from the surface. The alarms stopped, but there was another problem. Armstrong saw that their planned landing site was a crater full of boulders. He took manual control from the computer, and the Eagle skimmed along 100 metres above the surface of the moon. With fuel running out, Eagle urgently needed a safe place to land.

With only ninety seconds of fuel left, Armstrong spotted his landing place. About twenty metres above it, he slowed the rate of descent to roughly that of an elevator. Charlie Duke, who was speaking to the astronauts from Mission Control, cut in: 'Sixty seconds.' They had just a minute left in which to land. The Eagle's engine was blowing up moon dust that had been there for centuries.

3.16 pm Aldrin's voice was suddenly heard: 'Contact light!' This was the signal for Armstrong to shut down the engine, but he was so busy trying to fly that he forgot. There was a real danger that the running engine would blow up as Eagle landed – and this would have become a very different day in history.

3.17.43 pm In fact, Eagle settled so gently on the surface that the astronauts did not even feel the landing. An incredible moment in history had taken place. Exactly 102 hours, 45 minutes and 43 seconds after take-off, they had become the first men on the moon.

Armstrong sent back the message:
'Houston, the Eagle has landed.'

A Moment in Time

As the lunar module touches gently down on the moon, some 350,000 kilometres away on earth two reactions express the emotion of the moment. Mission Control in Houston, Texas, sends a relieved message to the astronauts: 'We copy you on the ground. You've got a bunch of guys about to turn blue [but] we're breathing again.' Nearly 2,000 kilometres from Houston, at Arlington Cemetery, Virginia, a well-wisher places a note on the memorial to ex-president John F Kennedy, who had kick-started the race to the moon before being assassinated in 1963. It reads: 'Mr President, the Eagle has landed.'

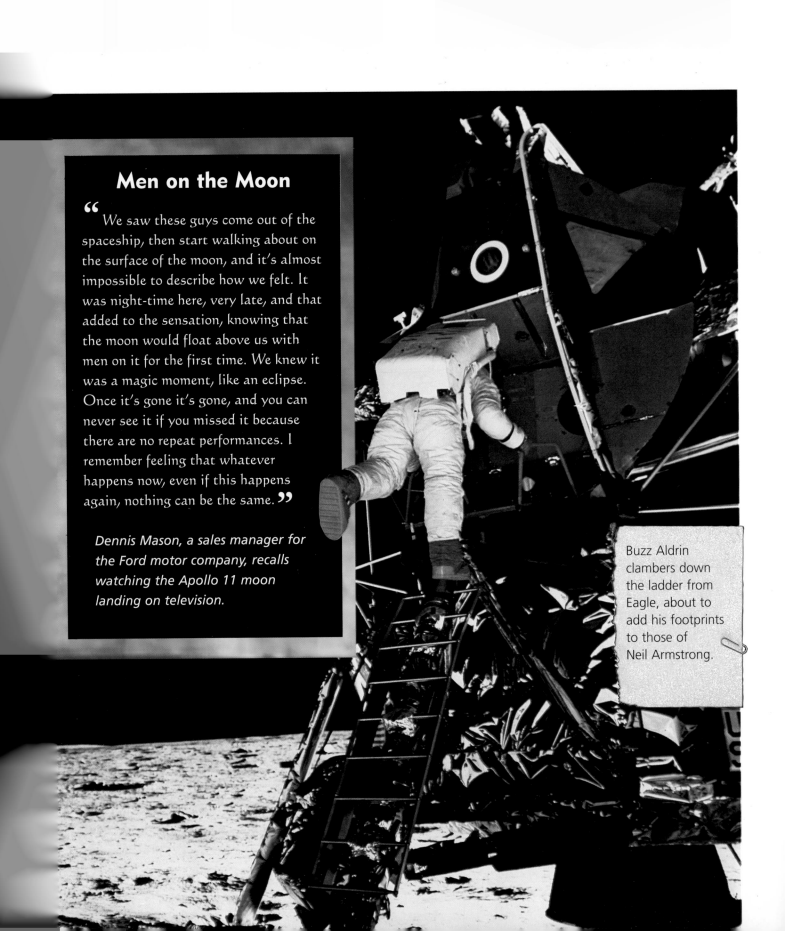

Men on the Moon

" We saw these guys come out of the spaceship, then start walking about on the surface of the moon, and it's almost impossible to describe how we felt. It was night-time here, very late, and that added to the sensation, knowing that the moon would float above us with men on it for the first time. We knew it was a magic moment, like an eclipse. Once it's gone it's gone, and you can never see it if you missed it because there are no repeat performances. I remember feeling that whatever happens now, even if this happens again, nothing can be the same. "

Dennis Mason, a sales manager for the Ford motor company, recalls watching the Apollo 11 moon landing on television.

Buzz Aldrin clambers down the ladder from Eagle, about to add his footprints to those of Neil Armstrong.

This famous photograph of Buzz Aldrin was taken by Neil Armstrong. You can see Armstrong reflected in the visor of Aldrin's helmet.

easy, and they radioed Houston to obtain permission to begin their moon walk earlier than planned.

7.21 pm The astronauts began to put on their spacesuits, a procedure that took over an hour. There is no atmosphere on the moon, so there was no oxygen for the astronauts to breathe. If they did not put the suits on properly, the moment they let the oxygen out of Eagle they would begin to suffocate.

9.28 pm After all the astronauts' careful preparations, the lunar module's door would not open – even though all the oxygen had been let out. Neither astronaut wanted to pull too hard on the door, for fear of damaging the thin metal. Finally, Aldrin pulled back a corner of the seal, and the door swung open. The two men were now standing in the airlessness of space, and below them was the reason for their journey – the surface of the moon.

Armstrong emerged from Eagle and stopped at the top of the escape ladder. He pulled a cord, and a small television camera fell into view at the side of the lunar module. A moment later, Armstrong heard a voice in his headset: 'We're getting a picture on the TV!' Viewers all round the world could now watch as Armstrong slowly descended the ladder. He paused on the bottom rung and his voice described to the world what he saw: 'The surface appears to be very, very fine-grained as you get close to it; it's almost like a powder.' Then he placed his foot on the moon's surface.

With one foot on the moon and the other on Eagle, Armstrong said: 'That's one small step for man ... one giant leap for mankind.'

3.18 pm Only seconds after the Eagle's engine had shut down, Armstrong and Aldrin immediately began the task of getting ready to leave the moon. In the event of an emergency they would need to take off quickly. This done, they tried to get some rest. But neither of them found this

9.42 pm Aldrin, who had spent the last fourteen minutes waiting alone in Eagle, radioed: 'Are you ready for me to come out?' Moments later, he too emerged into what he called the 'magnificent desolation' of the surface of the moon.

With Armstrong taking the photographs, Aldrin set up and saluted the American flag.

10.40 pm Armstrong and Aldrin unfurled an American flag. Because the moon has no atmosphere, there is no real wind on the surface – so the flag had been stiffened with wire to look as though it was flying in a breeze. The flagpole would only sink about twenty centimetres into the moon's hard rock, so the flag hung at a slightly odd angle. But this was the moment the USA had been waiting for. Whatever the angle, it was an American flag – not a Soviet one – that first flew on the moon.

With Armstrong operating the camera, Aldrin began to experiment with 'the various paces that a person can use travelling on the lunar surface'. He headed towards the camera at a slow jog, leaping about a metre with each stride. Suddenly a voice crackled through the ear-pieces worn by the astronauts. It was the president, Richard Nixon: 'Hello Neil and Buzz. I'm talking to you by telephone from the Oval Office of the White House ... I just can't tell you how proud we are of what you have done.'

Aldrin sets up one of the scientific experiments the astronauts would leave behind on the moon.

ONE OF THE FIRST things Neil Armstrong and Buzz Aldrin noticed as they walked about on the moon was its gravity, which is six times weaker than that of the earth. This allowed the astronauts to jump up and down, taking leaping steps with a feeling somewhere between walking and floating. On earth Armstrong and his spacesuit together had weighed 158 kilograms; here on the moon they weighed just 26 kilograms.

Neil Armstrong grins for the camera aboard Eagle, just after finishing his walk on the moon.

(**10.55 pm**) Aldrin inspected the Eagle ready for departure, while Armstrong collected soil and rock samples to be analysed by a team of geologists back home. These scientists were watching him on screen, feeling like children looking around a toyshop on closed-circuit television. Armstrong spent about ten minutes collecting their 'presents'.

(**11.39 pm**) The two astronauts set up the instruments they would leave behind on the moon's surface. The first was a seismometer, which would measure moonquakes. The second was a set of prisms that would act as a reflector for a laser beam from earth. This beam would allow scientists to measure the exact distance to the moon for the first time.

With time running short, Armstrong and Aldrin hurried through the rest of their work. Finally, they climbed back into Eagle and prepared for the long journey home. They left behind items including a gold olive branch to symbolize peace, and a tiny silicon disk bearing microscopic messages from the leaders of seventy-three countries.

A Moment in Time

At the same moment in time on the evening of 20 July 1969, 600 million people are staring at the same image. Two humans are walking on the surface of a different world, in the middle of space, and one-fifth of the earth's population gaze in wonder at their television screens. President Nixon is one of the viewers, and his message to the two astronauts is heard by the millions of others: 'For one priceless moment in the history of Man, all the peoples on this earth are truly one. One in their pride in what you have done, and one in our prayers that you will return safely to earth.'

As the three astronauts start the journey home, everyone in Mission Control waits with bated breath. The mission would only be a success if the astronauts returned safely.

ON THE MORNING OF Monday 21 July 1969, the lunar module rested on the moon's surface. The two astronauts inside were trying to sleep. Not surprisingly, they did not have much success. Over a hundred kilometres above them the Columbia command module was orbiting the moon under the control of Michael Collins. He had circled the moon every two hours for the last twenty hours. Now it was time to collect his fellow astronauts and take them home.

The launch of Eagle from the surface of the moon was the next vital and hazardous procedure. If the lunar module's rocket failed, the two astronauts would be left stranded on the moon to die. Their incredible achievement would be marred by tragedy. But if Aldrin was nervous, it hardly showed. Mission Control radioed the astronauts: 'You are cleared for take-off.' From the lonely surface of the moon,

Aldrin joked: 'Roger, understand. We're number one on the runway.'

At 12.54 pm, the countdown to take-off began: 'Nine, eight, seven, six, five, abort stage; engine arm, ascent; proceed.' Aldrin pushed the button. For a split second there was silence. It was followed by a muffled bang. Then came a smooth, even push as the ascent rocket worked perfectly, lifting Eagle smoothly away from the surface of the moon towards its rendezvous with Columbia.

As the Eagle came closer, Collins made the final delicate adjustments to Columbia's position. When he could, he also took photographs of the approaching spacecraft. One of them came out perfectly, with Eagle positioned between him and the distant planet earth. 'I got the earth coming up behind you,' he shouted. 'It's fantastic!' It is a photograph that captures an incredible moment in time – all humankind on earth, plus the two astronauts in Eagle. The only person not framed by the camera was Collins.

The two spacecraft docked successfully. After transferring their rock and soil samples, Armstrong and Aldrin tried to vacuum as much moon dust as they could from their spacesuits. This was not only about being neat and tidy – it was also part of the procedure to avoid the possibility of bringing germs back from the moon to the earth.

Armstrong and Aldrin left the lunar capsule and boarded Columbia to be reunited with Collins. Eagle was then jettisoned into space. It was left adrift in lunar orbit as the astronauts began their three-day journey back to earth.

A Moment in Time

At 12.50 pm, on the day after the first moon landing, Michael Collins is as alone as it is possible to be. He is in space orbiting the moon, the lone pilot of the spacecraft Columbia, as a moment that has haunted him approaches: 'My secret terror for the last six months has been leaving them on the moon and returning to earth alone; now I am within minutes of finding out the truth of the matter. If they fail to rise from the surface, or crash back into it, I am not going to commit suicide; I am coming home, forthwith, but I will be a marked man for life and I know it.'

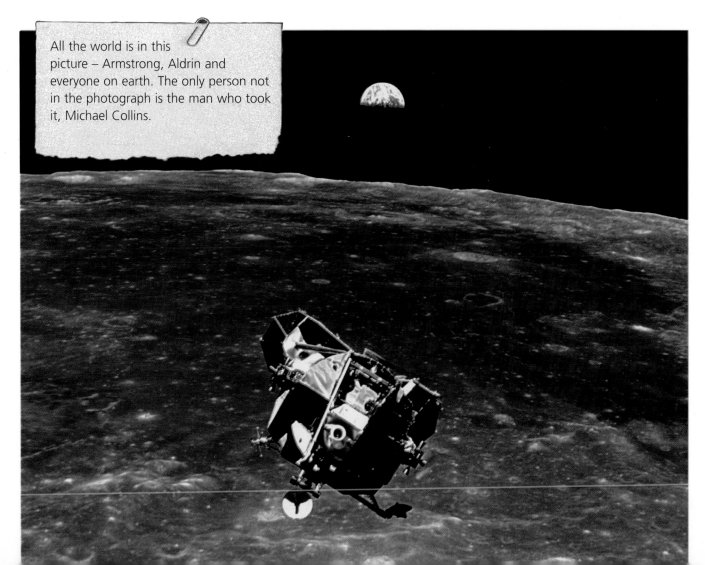

All the world is in this picture – Armstrong, Aldrin and everyone on earth. The only person not in the photograph is the man who took it, Michael Collins.

ON THURSDAY 24 JULY, four days after the moon landing, Columbia re-entered the earth's atmosphere. It was travelling at 39,750 kilometres per hour, and glowing with heat. As the capsule fell, three sets of parachutes opened to slow its descent. By the time the blackened spacecraft reached the surface of the sea, it was falling quite slowly, at just nine metres each second. The capsule splashed down in the Pacific, south-west of Hawaii. Having travelled 800,000 kilometres the astronauts landed just twenty kilometres from their recovery ship, the aircraft carrier *Hornet*. They were picked up by helicopter and flown to the ship, where President Nixon was waiting.

But if Nixon thought he would be able to shake their hands, he was wrong. At 1.16 pm, aboard the *Hornet*, the three astronauts took their first awkward steps under the effects of earth's gravity. They were dressed in grey 'biological isolation' suits with gas masks, and kept alone in a quarantine trailer.

Scientists were concerned that the astronauts might have brought back unknown germs from the moon.

It would be three weeks before the Apollo astronauts were allowed out to breathe the fresh air again, and to be reunited with their wives and families.

Armstrong, Aldrin and Collins returned from the moon to find that they had become national heroes. A grateful American public fêted them with a succession of parades and parties. Space became the most popular topic of conversation in school playgrounds and at dinner tables around the world. But things were about to change.

At one of the official celebrations for the Apollo 11 astronauts, someone (some people claim it was President Nixon) raised a glass to toast them and said: 'Here's to the Apollo programme. It's all over.' The speaker meant that the task John F Kennedy had set

Wearing isolation suits to keep the world safe from moon diseases, the three astronauts are recovered from Columbia after splashdown.

HORNET + 3

President Nixon enjoys a joke with the astronauts as they sit inside their quarantine capsule.

the USA in 1961 – to send a man to the moon and bring him safely home – had been accomplished. But the speaker was correct in another, more significant way. Some people said that you would not ask Lindbergh to fly across the Atlantic again, and nor was there any point in sending another mission to the moon. Further moon landings would in fact be made – but the world was changing fast and the achievement could never again be as glamorous or as popular as the flight of Apollo 11.

A Moment in Time

Safely aboard the *Hornet*, Aldrin, Armstrong and Collins sit and watch recordings showing the newspaper coverage of their mission. For the first time, they see the crowds gathered round television sets, amazed to be watching men walk on the moon. The astronauts suddenly sense the emotional impact of what they have achieved. While they were getting on with their job hundreds of thousands of kilometres away, the rest of the world had been spellbound. Aldrin, sensing the irony, turns to Armstrong and says: 'Neil, we missed the whole thing!'

Collins, Aldrin and Armstrong, in the back of an open-top limousine, enjoy a ticker-tape parade through New York on 13 August 1969.

The Apollo programme continues with the spectacular blast-off of Apollo 12.

NASA HAD ENOUGH FINANCIAL backing from the government to continue its programme of lunar exploration. It calculated that there were sufficient funds in the moon piggy-bank for nine more missions after Apollo 11, so the programme seemed likely to end with the flight of Apollo 20.

Apollo 12, which went to the moon in November 1969, was a great success. Astronauts Pete Conrad and Alan Bean spent over thirty-one hours on an area of the moon called the Ocean Of Storms. They managed to bring back almost twice as many moon rocks as Apollo 11, and even returned to earth with parts of Surveyor 3, an unmanned spacecraft which had been sent to the moon over two years before.

Popular culture showed how the '60s had become the 'space age'. In the days of the Mercury programme, enthusiasm for space had been reflected in the pop charts with hits like the Ventures' *Telstar*, which was named after the first satellite to beam live television pictures across the Atlantic. In the year of the moon landing, David Bowie first rocketed to stardom with *Space Oddity*, a haunting song about an astronaut adrift in space. In the cinemas in 1968 people had watched Stanley Kubrick's groundbreaking space movie *2001 – A Space Odyssey*. On television, Captain Kirk and the crew of *Star Trek* had been 'boldly going' to distant galaxies for three years by the time Armstrong walked on the moon.

But the '60s were coming to an end, and some people's attitudes to space exploration were changing. Not long after Apollo 12 returned, Apollo 20 was cancelled and Apollo 18 and 19 were put in doubt. An American flag now flew on the moon, so some people thought that the USA had already won the space race. Some members of the younger generation also

Captain Kirk, Doctor McCoy and Mr Spock, three of the characters from the original *Star Trek* television series which began in 1966 and ended in 1969.

A Moment in Time

In 1969, in the week in which Neil Armstrong and Buzz Aldrin walk on the moon, a futuristic song called *In the Year 2525*, by Zager and Evans, is the number one single in the American charts. It is not, as you might expect, a song celebrating the achievements of the astronauts. Instead, the song predicts a dull, lifeless future in which all human passions have been swept aside by technology.

associated the moon programme with the politicians who had led the USA into a war in Vietnam, in South-east Asia. The war was intended to confront and contain communism. But thousands of young Americans had died in the fighting, and by 1969 opposition to the war and to all things military was growing in the USA. It perhaps did not help that many of NASA's astronauts had military backgrounds.

Exactly a month after Apollo 11 had taken off, the Woodstock festival was taking place in New York. At this huge gathering of young music fans, members of the 'hippy' generation demonstrated their interest in music, peace and freedom. For some, space seemed less important than life on earth. As one of the performers Joni Mitchell wrote, they wanted to 'get back to the garden'.

Crowds enjoy the Woodstock music festival. Many of them were more interested in life on earth than exploring space.

EVEN WITHIN NASA ITSELF, some people felt that it was time to abandon moon exploration. Humans had been to the moon twice – what was the point of risking lives by sending further missions when there were other areas of space to explore? But in the face of such opposition, on 11 April 1970, Apollo 13 took off as planned.

At first everything went well. The launch was smooth, and for the first two days of the three-day journey to the moon the spacecraft worked perfectly. Then there was a loud bang, as one of the astronauts turned on a fan in the oxygen tanks.

A radio message was sent from the spacecraft: 'Okay, Houston; we've had a problem.'

They still had a problem, a big one. Although they did not know it yet, astronauts James Lovell, John Swigert and Fred Haise were facing a fight for their lives. Oxygen tank Number 2 had exploded when its fan was turned on. This had caused Apollo 13's other oxygen tank to burst its pipes and spill oxygen out of the side of the spacecraft. Soon the command module was virtually useless, and the astronauts were forced to move through into the lunar module, named Aquarius, which should have been used for the moon landing. It was not designed to support three astronauts, and they had to use minimal power.

Low on oxygen and fuel, the astronauts nursed their spacecraft the rest of the way to the moon, around the lunar orbit and back towards earth. Once again, the

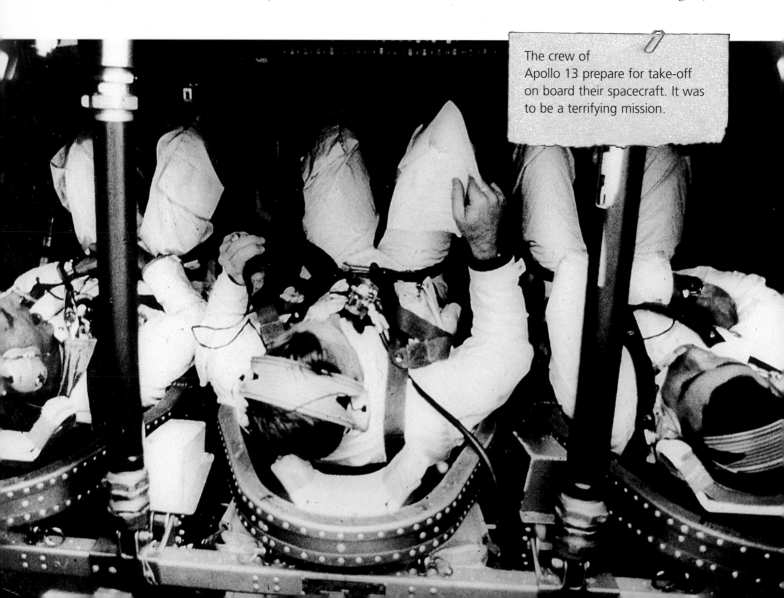

The crew of Apollo 13 prepare for take-off on board their spacecraft. It was to be a terrifying mission.

President Nixon joins the crew of Apollo 13 at a ceremony to honour their achievement in guiding their damaged spacecraft back to earth.

drama of the space race caught the attention of millions of people. During the whole journey the world held its breath, waiting to see if the astronauts could survive against all the odds aboard the ruined capsule. They did make it back safely, splashing down in the Pacific Ocean on 17 April 1970. NASA official Robert Gilruth said that Apollo 13 had been a frightening reminder that 'flying to the moon is not just a bus ride'.

President Nixon visited NASA not long afterwards, awarding medals to the flight controllers who had helped save the Apollo 13 astronauts. But the political climate was changing, and the White House had already let it be known that space was no longer a national priority.

Space Values

" I believe it would be unconscionable to embark on a project of such staggering cost when many of our citizens are malnourished, when our rivers and lakes are polluted, and when our cities and rural areas are dying. What are our values? What do we think more important? "

Congressman Walter Mondale objects to NASA's budget in the summer of 1970. The budget was approved, but Tom Paine – the head of NASA since its creation – resigned, leaving the battles for funding to his successor.

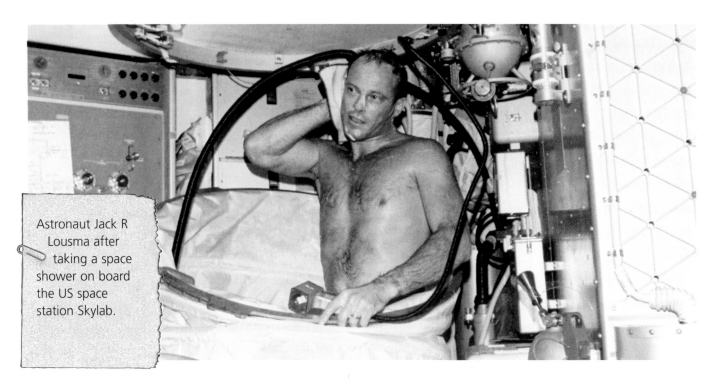

Astronaut Jack R Lousma after taking a space shower on board the US space station Skylab.

THE APOLLO MISSIONS ENDED more with a whimper than a bang. By the time Apollo 17 splashed down on 19 December 1972, the public's former fascination with space had faded. In both the USA and the Soviet Union people questioned the benefits of spending vast amounts of money on sending men to the moon.

Despite misgivings about finance, NASA pressed ahead with a project called Skylab. This was a laboratory in space, circling the earth in a low orbit. Skylab was home to three missions between 1973 and 1974, the last of which stayed in space for eighty-four days. At the same time, the Soviet Union continued to explore space through the Salyut series of space stations. There were seven of these, and they were reached by astronauts travelling in Soyuz spacecraft.

In 1975, history was made when the Soviet Union and the USA co-operated in space for the first time. On 17 July the last Apollo spacecraft ever launched docked with a Soviet Soyuz spacecraft. During the next two days the crews made four transfers and conducted five joint experiments. Despite this joint mission, the two superpowers continued to develop their own space programmes independently, and during the early 1980s the rivalries between the two countries became more intense once again.

Star Wars

In the 1980s, American president Ronald Reagan approved development of the Strategic Defense Initiative (SDI), known as 'Star Wars'. SDI was designed to protect the USA from nuclear attack, using defence systems mounted on satellites. The huge costs involved and the end of the Cold War meant that Star Wars was never fully developed – but plans were reawakened in 2001 under President George W Bush.

Public interest in space was rekindled on 12 April 1981, when the American space shuttle Columbia took off from the Kennedy Space Center in Florida. The shuttle returned from space to land successfully at Edwards Air Force Base two days later. The USA now had a reusable spacecraft, which could ferry materials into space, return safely, and prepare to launch again.

On 20 February 1986, the Soviet Union launched Mir, a new space station. *Mir* means 'peace' in Russian, and it was Mir that was to show the first signs of an end to the battle in space. This reflected the thawing of the Cold War here on earth. In 1989, the Berlin Wall in Germany, which divided East and West Berlin and had become the most striking symbol of the divide between communism and democracy, was torn down. Two years later, the Soviet Union broke up, and the Mir space station came under the direction of the Russian Federation. Russia signed agreements with the USA for Mir and the space shuttle to be used together. Several American astronauts visited Mir in the following years, helping to develop the technology that would assist in the development of an international space station.

The space shuttle launches from the Kennedy Space Center.

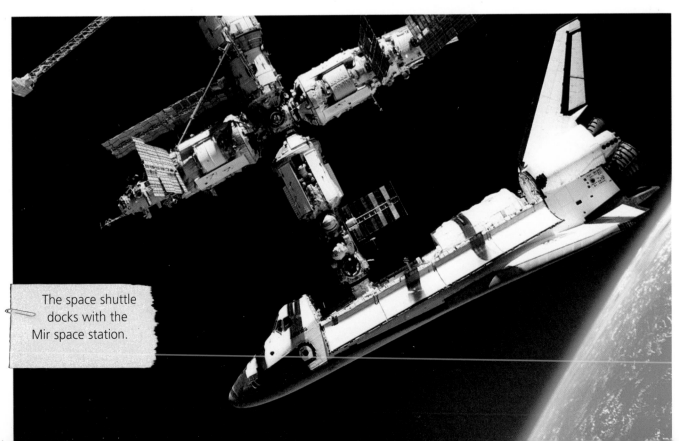

The space shuttle docks with the Mir space station.

WHAT IF, ON 20 July 1969, Apollo 11 had not landed on the moon? What would the world be like if there had been no space race at all? One way to try to answer this question is to look at some of the things that were developed to help the quest to reach the moon.

Try to imagine a world without any of the technology produced for Apollo. People who suffer from certain heart problems do not have pacemakers to keep their heartbeat regular. Buildings have no smoke detectors to warn of a potentially fatal fire. There are no coatings to produce scratch-resistant spectacles. Pens that write when they are upside-down do not exist. Athletes curse their sore feet, because they do not have the comfort of the shock-absorbers found in the soles of modern running shoes. The cordless drill has never been invented. There are also longer queues in the supermarket because none of the products are marked with a bar-code!

Of course, some or all of these things might eventually have been developed anyway. But they became part of people's lives at the time they did because they had been created as part of the space programme.

The moon landing also suggested that anything was possible if it was attempted with sufficient determination and resources. Spacecraft now travel from earth to distant planets, and the pictures from their cameras are transmitted to the computer screens of ordinary people through the internet. Had Apollo 11 ended in disaster, future generations might never have attempted to reach for such seemingly impossible goals. John F Kennedy summed this up when he began the race to the moon in 1961: 'We choose to go to the

The space shuttle Challenger moments after it exploded on 28 January 1986, killing all seven members of the crew. Would space travel still have been attempted if Apollo 11 had ended in similar tragedy?

One of the great lessons humanity can learn from the race to the moon is just how beautiful our own planet is.

moon and do the other things, not because they are easy but because they are hard. Because that goal will serve to organize and measure the best of our skill and energy.'

In the end, Apollo's greatest achievement may have been one that was never planned. By travelling to the moon, people were able to see the earth properly for the first time. The picture of the 'big blue marble' floating in space contrasted with what Buzz Aldrin had called the 'magnificent desolation' of the moon. Without this perspective, people might never have realized what an amazing planet they live on. The Apollo 8 astronaut William Anders put it best: 'We came all this way to explore the moon, and the most important thing is that we discovered the earth.'

Cool Inventions

There were other, more unusual things that NASA pioneered for its moon missions. The technology used to keep the Apollo capsules floating the right way up after splashdown is now used in a self-righting life-raft that has saved over 500 lives. Underwear that kept the astronauts from getting too hot in their spacesuits has been adapted for use by racing drivers and nuclear reactor technicians. Four hundred of these 'cool suits' were also used in the Gulf War.

The International Space Station, which is now in orbit around the earth.

SPACE EXPLORATION DID NOT end with the last Apollo landing on the moon. Scientists have continued to explore further and further from the earth, sending out probes to cover the vast distances to other worlds in the hope of finding out more about the Universe. Unlike the Apollo spacecraft, these probes are unmanned. Because of the huge amount of time it takes to reach distant planets, astronauts cannot make the journey. The probes send back data automatically for analysis on earth.

One of the most amazing programmes was carried out by NASA's Voyager probes, launched in 1977. They visited Jupiter, Saturn, Uranus and Neptune, sending information back to earth as they travelled. The distances involved are such that when Voyager 2 reached Neptune in 1989 it had been travelling for twelve years.

By 1997 the USA's Pathfinder robot was exploring the surface of Mars, sending back images that could be watched on the internet. Millions of people were able to study the 'red planet' from their own homes, and felt something of the excitement experienced by those who had watched television pictures of the moon landing nearly thirty years before.

Today the exploration of space is much more about co-operation between countries than rivalries like the one that spawned the race to the moon. The best example of this is the International Space Station (ISS), which is the result of sixteen nations working together. When the ISS is finished, it will be four times bigger than the Mir space station. The first phase opened in 2000, and is in orbit 400 kilometres above the surface of the earth. From here it can observe 85% of the earth's surface and 95% of the world's people. The first crew of the ISS included both Russian and American astronauts.

In the nineteenth century, works of fiction predicted the first journey to the moon. Today, films and books predict a future world of space travel and extraterrestrial life. Already, the introduction of reusable spacecraft is making it possible for ordinary people to share the experience of the Apollo astronauts. In 1984, NASA introduced the 'Space Flight Participant' programme, which planned for teachers, artists and others to travel in space. Senator John Glenn joined a shuttle flight in 1998 at the age of seventy-seven. In 2001, American millionaire Dennis Tito became the

A Moment in Time

As Neil Armstrong steps from the lunar module on 20 July 1969, his boot makes a footprint in the ancient dust that lies on the moon's surface. There is no atmosphere on the moon, so no wind will ever disturb the marks of this footprint.

world's first space tourist, after paying to join a Russian flight to the ISS.

People are now living and working in space stations, and scientists predict there will one day be a colony on the moon. This may seem like fiction, but then so did a journey from the earth to the moon. It would certainly be an extraordinary legacy of Neil Armstrong's 'giant leap' for mankind.

A group of shuttle astronauts in 1998. The US senator John Glenn, far right, became the first American into orbit in 1962, then, at the age of 77, went back into space.

Glossary

aeronautical   To do with the science of navigating in the air.

aerospace   To do with flight in the earth's atmosphere and in space.

atmosphere   The gases surrounding a planet such as earth.

atomic bomb   A bomb of immense destructive power, created through the energy that is released when atoms are split.

capitalist   A person who believes in capitalism, the system used in countries such as Britain and the USA which encourages private ownership and profit.

celestial body   Any piece of matter in the sky, such as a planet, sun, moon or star.

Cold War   The period of history between about 1949 and 1989 when the USA and its allies were enemies with the Soviet Union and its allies. It was known as the Cold War because the two sides never fought each other in the heat of an actual battle.

command module   The part of an Apollo spacecraft that orbited the moon, waiting for the lunar module to return.

communist   Someone who believes in communism, the system used in the Soviet Union which states that capitalism is harmful and that all property should be publicly owned.

Congress   The body of officials who make the laws in the USA.

dark side of the moon   The part of the moon's surface that cannot be seen from earth.

democratic   Practising democracy, the system where a country is governed by all of its people, through a fairly elected government.

dock   Link two spacecraft together, usually to allow people or goods to be transferred from one to the other.

eclipse   When a celestial body, such as the moon, blocks out the light of another body, such as the sun.

geologists   Scientists who study the formation of rocks on the earth or moon.

Korean War   The war fought from 1950 to 1953 between communist North Korea and forces, including many American soldiers, defending South Korea.

Kremlin   The buildings in Moscow that housed the Soviet government.

lunar   To do with the moon.

lunar module   The part of an Apollo spaceship that detached from the command module and flew to the surface of the moon.

malnourished   Not having enough food to be healthy.

Mission Control   The facility and people who controlled the Apollo flights from their base in Houston, Texas.

NASA   National Aeronautics and Space Administration, the organization that has run the USA's space programme since 1958.

Nazi   A member of the Nazi party, a political party that started in Germany during the 1920s. The Nazis ruled Germany from 1933 to 1944, under Adolf Hitler, who led the country into the Second World War.

orbit   The circular or elliptical path one body takes around another.

Oval Office   The American president's office in the White House.

prisms Specially shaped devices of solid glass or quartz used to change the direction of a beam of light. They are used in lenses and for measuring light.

probes Unmanned exploratory spacecraft that transmit information.

quarantine When somebody or something is kept in isolation for a period of time to prevent the spread of disease.

respiration Breathing.

rocketry The science of rockets.

satellite A heavenly body orbiting a planet (the moon is a satellite of the earth); or a machine sent into space to orbit a planet.

seismometer An instrument used to measure the force of earthquakes.

simulator In the space programme, a simulator was a copy of a spacecraft in which the astronauts practised for their missions.

Soviet Union Sometimes called the Union of Soviet Socialist Republics or USSR, the Soviet Union occupied a large area of Eastern Europe and Asia from 1917 to 1990.

sub-orbital Not completing a full orbit of the earth.

superpowers The name given to the two most powerful nations in the world, the Soviet Union and the USA, during the Cold War.

tyranny The cruel and unjust use of power by a ruler.

unconscionable Without a conscience, immoral.

White House The official home of the American president in Washington.

Further Information

Reading

Armstrong Lands On The Moon by Gordon Charleston (Zoe Books, 1994)
Moon Landing: The Race For The Moon by Carole Stott (Dorling Kindersley, 1999)
Space Exploration by Carole Stott (Dorling Kindersley, 1997)

Sources

A Man On The Moon: The Voyages of the Apollo Astronauts (Penguin, 1994).
A detailed, fascinating look at the history of the Apollo programme, with a foreword by actor and space buff Tom Hanks.
One Small Step: Project Apollo and the Legacy of the Space Age by Eugene Fowler (Smithmark Publishers, 1999).
Excellent photos and a clear, brief text.

Films

Apollo 13 directed by Ron Howard (1995)
The Right Stuff directed by Philip Kaufman (1983)

Websites

www.nasa.gov
Some of the best space websites belong to NASA.
www.ksc.nasa.gov
The Kennedy Space Center website.
www.spaceflight.nasa.gov
The International Space Centre home page is also a home page for the space shuttle.
www.bbc.co.uk
The BBC has a good short section on the moon landings.
Visit learn.co.uk for more resources.

Timeline

1926 The American Robert Goddard launches the first ever liquid-fuelled rocket.

1933 The Nazi Party comes to power in Germany. Robert Ley, a key member of the German Rocket Society, leaves for the USA. Wernher von Braun, another leading member, is put to work designing rocket-powered weapons for the German military. A Soviet scientist named Sergei Korolev launches a rocket 400 metres into the sky. Three months later, a Soviet rocket reaches a height of five kilometres.

1935 Robert Goddard launches a rocket that flies 2.3 kilometres into the air.

3 October 1942 Germany's first V2 rocket-powered bomb is launched at London from the Baltic coast.

May 1945 Germany surrenders and Wernher von Braun and his team of rocket scientists go to the USA to work for the US Army.

August 1945 The USA drops atomic bombs on Hiroshima and Nagasaki in Japan.

1949 The Soviet Union develops its own atomic bomb.

1955–8 The Soviet Union and the USA develop long-range, rocket-powered weapons capable of carrying an atomic bomb hundreds of kilometres.

4 October 1957 The Soviet Union launches the satellite Sputnik 1 into orbit around the earth.

November 1957 The Soviet Union launches Sputnik 2, which carries Laika the dog into orbit.

December 1957 The US Navy's attempt to launch a Vanguard rocket carrying a satellite fails. The rocket explodes on the launch pad.

1 October 1958 NASA, the USA's organizing body for rocket research and space travel, is formed.

12 April 1961 Yuri Gagarin, a Soviet astronaut, becomes the first human in space, travelling aboard Sputnik 3.

25 May 1961 The new US president, John F Kennedy, commits the USA to trying to put a man on the moon by the end of the 1960s.

February 1962 John Glenn becomes the first American astronaut in orbit around the earth.

June 1966 Astronaut Ed White performs the first American space walk.

27 January 1967 Apollo 1 explodes on the launch pad during a test, killing the three astronauts inside.

9 November 1967 The first Saturn 5 rocket, which will eventually power the moon missions, is launched.

21–28 December 1968 Apollo 8 makes the first flight around the moon.

16–24 July 1969 Apollo 11 makes a successful visit to the moon. Astronauts Neil Armstrong and Buzz Aldrin walk on the moon's surface on 20 July 1969.

11–17 April 1970 Apollo 13 makes a disastrous attempt to land on the moon. An oxygen tank explodes on the spacecraft, and the three astronauts aboard are lucky to return to earth alive.

7–19 December 1972 Apollo 17, the last Apollo mission, makes the final visit to the moon.

Neil Armstrong's footprint on the moon's surface, preserved for all time.

Index

Numbers in **bold** refer
to illustrations.

Aldrin, Edwin 'Buzz' 6, **6**, 17, 20,
  21, 23, 24, 25, 26, **26**, 27, **27**, 28,
  28, 29, 30, 31, 33, **33**, 35, 41
Anders, William A 18, **19**, 41
Apollo programme 18, 34, 35, 36,
  37, 38, 40, 41
Apollo 1: 18
Apollo 4: 18
Apollo 7: 18, **18**
Apollo 8: 18, 19, **19**, 20, 41
Apollo 9: 18
Apollo 10: 18
Apollo 11:
  astronauts 20, 21, **21**
  lift-off 7, **7**, 22, **22**, 23, **23**
  moon landing 25, **25**, 26, **26**, 27,
    27, 28, **28**, 29
  scientific experiments **28**, 29, 31
  splashdown 32, **32**
  technology 40, 41
Apollo 12: 34, **34**
Apollo 13: 36, **36**, 37, **37**
Apollo 17: 38
Armstrong, Neil 6, **6**, 20, **20**, 21,
  21, 23, 24, 25, 27, **27**, 28, 29, **29**,
  31, 33, **33**, 34, 35, 43
atomic bomb 10, **10**, 11, 38

Berlin Wall 39
Braun, Wernher von 9, **9**, 12,
  13, 17
Bumper **11**
Bush, George W 38

Challenger **40**
Churchill, Winston 11
Cold War 11, 38, 39
Collins, Michael 6, **6**, 20, **21**, 23,
  24, 30, 31, 33, **33**
Columbia (command module) 24,
  24, 30, 31, 32
Columbia (space shuttle) 39
Corporal **11**

docking 16, **17**, 20, 23, 31, 38
Duke, Charlie 25

Eagle (lunar module) 24, **24**, 25,
  26, 27, 29, 30, 31, **31**
earth 18, 19, 30, **31**, 41, **41**
Eisenhower, Dwight D 12, **13**, 14

Freedom 7: 15

Gagarin, Yuri 15, **15**, 17
Gemini programme 16, 17, **17**
German Rocket Society 9
Glenn, John 16, 43, **43**
Goddard, Robert 8, **8**, 9, 10
gravity 22, 28, 32

Hornet 32, 33, **33**

ICBM 11, 12
In the Year 2525: 35
internet 40, 42
Iron Curtain 11
ISS **42**, 43

Johnson, Lyndon B 22, **22**

Kennedy, John F 14, 15, 16, **16**, 17,
  25, 32, 40
Kennedy Space Center 6, 7, 8, **11**,
  39, **39**
Khrushchev, Nikita **13**
Korean War 14, 21
Korolev, Sergei 10, **11**

Laika 12, 13, **13**
Ley, Robert 9
Lindbergh, Charles 21, 33
Lovell, James A 18, 36
Luna programme 16

Mars 42
Mercury programme 14, **14**, 16, 34
Mir 39, **39**, 43
Mission Control **16**, 22, 24, 25, **25**,
  30, **30**

NASA 6, 13, 14, 15, 16, **16**, 18, 20,
  21, 34, 35, 36, 37, 38, 41, 42, 43
Nazi Germany 9, 17
'New Frontier' 15
Nixon, Richard 28, 29, 32, **33**,
  37, **37**

Pathfinder 42
pop music 34, 35
probe 13, 42

quarantine 32, **33**

R-7: 12
Reagan, Ronald 38
rocket development 8, 9, 10, 11,
  12, 13, 17

Salyut 38
satellite 10, 12, 38
Saturn 5: 7, **7**, 17, 18, 22
SDI 38
Second World War 9, 10, 11,
  12, 14
Shepard, Alan 15, **15**, 16
Skylab 38, **38**
Soyuz 38
Space Oddity 34
space shuttle 39, **39**, 40, 43
space station 38, **39**, **42**, 43
space walk 16
Sputnik 1: 10, 12, **12**
Sputnik 2: 13
Star Trek 34, 35
Surveyor 3: 34

television 7, 18, 22, 23, 26, 27, 29,
  33, 34, 42
Tito, Dennis 43
2001 – A Space Odyssey 34

V2: 9, **11**, 17
Vanguard 12, 13
Verne, Jules 8
Vietnam War 35
Vostok 15
Voyager programme 42

weapons 9, 10, 11, 12, 38
White, Ed 16, 18
Woodstock 35, **35**